the
Whole Grain
COOKBOOK

Over 50 quick and easy whole grain recipes

Created and produced by Ivy Contract
Consultant Judith Wills
Photography by Clive Streeter
Food styling by Angela Drake

Notes for the Reader
This book uses imperial, metric, and US cup measurements. Follow the same units of measurement throughout; do not mix imperial and metric. All spoon measurements are level: teaspoons are assumed to be 5 ml, and tablespoons are assumed to be 15 ml. Unless otherwise stated, milk is assumed to be whole, eggs and individual vegetables, such as potatoes, are medium, and pepper is freshly ground black pepper.

The times given are an approximate guide only. Preparation times differ according to the techniques used by different people and the cooking times may also vary from those given as a result of the type of oven used. Optional ingredients, variations, or serving suggestions have not been included in the calculations.

Recipes using raw or very lightly cooked eggs should be avoided by infants, the elderly, pregnant women, convalescents, and anyone with a chronic condition. Pregnant and breastfeeding women are advised to avoid eating peanuts and peanut products. People with nut allergies should be aware that some of the store-bought ingredients used in the recipes in this book may contain nuts. Always check the packaging before use.

Picture Acknowledgments
The publisher would like to thank the following for permission to reproduce copyright material: Maximilian Stock Ltd/PhotoCuisine/Corbis (front cover, top right) and Getty Images (pages 7, 8, 28, 64, and 102).

Contents

Introduction

Recently published figures show that we are finally getting the message that we should eat at least five portions of fruit and vegetables a day. But did you know that it is just as important to get your daily whole grains? Just three portions of whole grain foods a day are all you need to get the benefits—so it's surprising that nine out of ten of us don't eat that much.

Whole grains are foods such as whole wheat breakfast cereals, whole wheat pasta, and whole wheat bread. We now know that these foods can make a major contribution to our well-being by keeping our hearts healthy, helping us to get—or stay—slim, and by helping to keep the digestive system in good order.

Start your own 3-a-day whole grain diet and see how easy it is to eat the servings your body needs. Begin by trying the delicious recipes in this book—incorporate them into your diet and you will easily make your 3-a-day, every day!

KEY TO THE INFORMATION BOXES USED IN THIS BOOK

 Whole grain per serving: The number of whole grain portions per single serving.

Serves: The number of people each recipe serves.

 Prep. time: The time it takes to prepare and cook the recipe (excludes overnight soaking, marinating, or thawing).

Regularly eating whole grains can help all the family to better health. Several major studies have found they can help reduce the risk of strokes, heart disease, type 2 diabetes, certain cancers, digestive problems, asthma, obesity, and gum disease. They are also rich in nutrients, such as B vitamins, iron, and magnesium.

Whole grains for a healthy family

What it is

Any type of grain, such as wheat, rice, oats, rye, barley, or corn, in its whole, unrefined, natural form is whole grain. Whole grains contain all three parts of the grain—the nutrient-rich germ, the energy-providing endosperm, and the fiber-rich bran layer. When grains are refined to make white flour, white rice, or white bread, for example, the outer bran layer and germ of the grain are stripped away, resulting in the loss of much of the fiber and some of the nutrients.

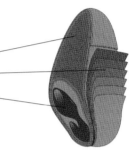

Whole grain kernel
Endosperm: makes up 83% of the kernel
Bran: makes up 14% of the kernel
Germ: makes up 3% of the kernel
(percentages are approximate)

What is a whole grain food?

Whole grain foods include whole wheat bread, whole wheat pasta, bulgar wheat, brown rice, shredded wheat biscuits, and oatmeal.

What portion sizes provide one whole grain serving?

- 1 medium slice (1 oz/30 g) whole wheat bread
- 1 small slice (¾ oz/20 g) dark rye bread
- 1 mini whole wheat pita or half a standard whole wheat pita
- 3 heaping tbsp (3 oz/90 g) cooked whole wheat pasta
- 2 tbsp (scant 3 oz/80 g) cooked brown rice
- 1 shredded whole wheat biscuit
- 2 round oatcakes
- scant ⅓ cup (¾ oz/20 g) rolled oats (raw weight) or whole grain flakes
- 1 small bowlful (¾ oz/20 g) whole grain breakfast cereal
- heaping 1 tbsp (¾ oz/20 g) whole wheat flour

whole grain recipes

Providing the family with nutritious and tasty whole grain meals doesn't mean you have to spend lots of time struggling with complicated or lengthy recipes.

The simple methods in this book can guide even the most inexperienced cooks to make a wide variety of tempting dishes for breakfast, lunch, dinner, and dessert. The whole family will enjoy creating and eating these mouth-watering meals.

Yes—you really can make delicious and healthy whole grain recipes, such as **Sticky Salmon with Noodles** for dinner or **Sweet Peach Delight** for dessert. Have a look through this book and see what you could make today!

brilliant
breakfasts

diy muesli

½ cup rolled oats
heaping ½ cup barley or rye flakes
2 shredded wheat biscuits, crushed
scant ¼ cup shelled Brazil nuts, coarsely chopped
scant ¼ cup shelled hazelnuts
¼ cup sunflower seeds
generous ¼ cup chopped plumped dried apricots
2 red apples, cored and coarsely chopped, to serve
⅔ cup skim or lowfat milk, to serve

❶ Mix together all the muesli ingredients in a large bowl (see Tips).

❷ When ready to serve, divide the muesli among the serving dishes.

❸ Serve with the apples and milk.

⭐ *Tips: You can vary the nuts, seeds, and dried fruits to make a change. Store in an airtight container in a cool place and the muesli will keep for a few weeks, so double or quadruple quantities to make more.*

Whole grain per serving **2** | Serves **4** | Prep time **5 mins**

hunger buster oatmeal crunch

1¼ cups rolled oats
2 cups water
¼ tsp salt
2 tbsp chopped plumped dried apricots
2 tbsp toasted slivered almonds
4 tsp sunflower seeds

❶ Mix the oats with the water and salt in a nonstick saucepan and stir well. Bring to a boil over medium–high heat, stirring occasionally, then reduce the heat and simmer, continuing to stir occasionally, for 5 minutes.

❷ When the oatmeal is thick and creamy, spoon into 2 serving bowls and top with the apricots, almonds, and sunflower seeds (see Tip).

⭐ *Tip: You can vary the dried fruits, nuts, and seeds that you use in this hearty breakfast. They all contain an excellent range of vitamins and minerals. Try serving with ⅔ cup skim or lowfat milk.*

Whole grain per serving
2.5

Prep. time
15mins

swiss-style muesli

⅔ cup skim or lowfat milk, plus extra for serving
2½ cups rolled oats
2 shredded wheat biscuits, crushed
⅔ cup apple juice
2 red apples, cored and coarsely chopped
1 tbsp light brown sugar
4 tbsp chopped mixed nuts

❶ Put the milk into a saucepan and cook over medium heat until warm but not boiling, or put into a microwavable pitcher or bowl and heat on high in the microwave for 1 minute (see Tips).

❷ Pour the oats, shredded wheat, and half the apple juice into a pitcher or bowl with the milk, stirring thoroughly. Cover and let soak for at least 3 hours or overnight at room temperature.

❸ When ready to serve, mix the apples, sugar, nuts, and the remaining apple juice into the oat and shredded wheat mixture (see Tips). Serve with a little extra warm or cold milk.

Tips: Heating times for the milk vary according to microwave wattage, as follows: 800W—0.5 minutes; 750W—1 minute; 650W—1.5 minutes. The muesli should taste rich and creamy—rather like a cold "oatmeal." You can top the muesli with extra fresh fruit, such as sliced kiwi or orange.

Whole grain per serving 3 | Serves 4 | Prep time 10mins

hot tropical oatmeal

scant 1¼ cups rolled oats
1¼ cups hot water
pinch of salt
2 tbsp tropical fruit and nut mix
1 large or 2 small bananas
⅔ cup reduced-fat coconut milk, to serve (see Tip)

❶ Put the oats into a nonstick saucepan and add the hot water and salt. Stir well and bring to a boil, then reduce the heat and simmer, stirring often, for 5 minutes, until the oatmeal is thick and fairly smooth.

❷ When the oatmeal is nearly ready, stir in the tropical fruit and nut mix and cook for an additional minute.

❸ Spoon the oatmeal into 2 serving bowls. Peel the banana and slice it over the top. Serve immediately with reduced-fat coconut milk.

⭐ *Tip: Cans of reduced-fat coconut milk can be bought from most supermarkets.*

Whole grain per serving	Serves	Prep. time
2.5	2	10 mins

mixed berry crêpes

1½ cups mixed berries, such as raspberries, strawberries,
  and blackberries
2 tbsp superfine sugar
2 tbsp water
⅔ cup whole wheat flour
1 tsp baking powder
pinch of salt
2 small eggs
½ cup lowfat or skim milk
sunflower oil, for brushing
⅔ cup thick plain yogurt

❶ Put 1 cup of the berries, 1 tablespoon of the sugar, and the water into a saucepan and simmer for 4–5 minutes, until there is a rich juice and the berries are slightly soft.

❷ Meanwhile, combine the flour, baking powder, and salt in a bowl. Beat the eggs with the remaining sugar in another bowl until pale, then add the milk and beat again. Finally, add the flour mixture and beat until smooth.

❸ Brush a medium, heavy-bottom, nonstick skillet with oil and heat. Spoon half the crêpe batter into the skillet. Cook over high heat for 2 minutes, until the underside is golden. Flip over and cook for an additional minute. Cook the remaining batter in the same way. Serve with the cooked berries, topped with the remaining fresh berries and the yogurt.

Whole grain per serving	Serves	Prep. time
2.5	2	15mins

pineapple and banana smoothie

1 large banana
generous 1 cup pineapple juice
generous ¾ cup thick plain yogurt with honey
2 heaping tbsp fine oatmeal

❶ Peel and chop the banana, put it into a blender with the pineapple juice, and process for about 30 seconds, until smooth.

❷ Add the yogurt and oatmeal and process again for a few seconds, until thickened. Pour into 2 glasses and chill (see Tip).

⭐ *Tip: This smoothie will thicken if left to stand, because of the oatmeal. It can then be eaten with a spoon, like a yogurt.*

Whole grain per serving
1

Serves
2

Prep. time
3mins

strawberry breakfast dip

¾ cup ripe strawberries, hulled and coarsely chopped,
   plus extra to garnish
1 tbsp confectioners' sugar
generous ¾ cup cream cheese
1 tsp lemon juice
4 slices whole wheat bread
2 large pieces of fruit, such as a mango, nectarine, or banana,
   cut into wedges

❶ Process the strawberries together with the confectioners'
sugar in a blender for a few seconds or mash with the sugar
using a fork.

❷ Combine the mixture with the cream cheese and lemon juice
in a bowl. Spoon into a serving dish and chill, if you have time.

❸ Toast the bread and cut into strips. Arrange the fruit as
dippers on a plate around the strawberry dip. Garnish the dip
with half a fresh strawberry (see Tip).

⭐ *Tip: The dip is also nice topped with fresh fruit and whole grain cereal
and eaten with a spoon.*

Whole grain per serving		Prep. time
1		10mins

ham and egg feast

2 eggs
2 tsp lowfat spread or olive oil spread, plus extra to serve
3½ oz/100 g mushrooms, thinly sliced
2 slices whole wheat bread
2¾ oz/80 g wafer-thin slices of ham
salt and pepper

❶ Break the eggs into a saucepan of simmering water and poach for 3–5 minutes, until the whites have set (see Tip).

❷ Meanwhile, melt the lowfat spread in a small nonstick skillet and stir-fry the mushrooms over low heat. Toast the bread.

❸ Spread the toast with lowfat spread and top with the ham. Using a slotted spoon, remove the eggs from the pan and place 1 egg on each slice of toast. Spoon the mushrooms on top, season to taste with salt and pepper, and serve immediately.

⭐ *Tip: For young children and the elderly, make sure that the eggs are thoroughly cooked.*

Whole grain per serving	Serves	Prep. time
1	2	10 mins

eggs florentine

4 eggs
9 oz/250 g baby spinach leaves, chopped
4 tbsp light cream
2 whole wheat English muffins
salt and pepper

❶ Break the eggs into a saucepan of simmering water and poach for 3–5 minutes, until the whites have set.

❷ Place the spinach in a saucepan with just the water clinging to the leaves and cook over medium–high heat, stirring, for up to 3 minutes, or place the leaves in a microwavable bowl and heat on high in the microwave for 1 minute, or until wilted (see Tip). Mix in the cream, a little salt, and plenty of black pepper.

❸ When the eggs are cooked to your liking, remove them from the pan with a slotted spatula or spoon and put them, still in the spoon, on paper towels to drain thoroughly.

❹ Slice the muffins in half horizontally before toasting. Top each toasted slice with a quarter of the spinach mixture, and put an egg on top. Serve immediately, seasoned with a little extra black pepper.

⭐ *Tip: Cooking times for the spinach vary according to microwave wattage, as follows: 800W—0.5 minutes; 750W—1 minute; 650W—1.5 minutes. If using ready-washed spinach, add 1 tablespoon of water to the bowl before cooking.*

Whole grain per serving **2**   Prep. time **10 mins**

yummy
lunches

chicken satay sandwich

2 heaping tbsp crunchy peanut butter
3 tbsp thick plain yogurt
5½ oz/150 g cooked Thai- or Chinese-style chicken strips
4 slices whole wheat bread
cucumber strips and salad greens, to serve

❶ Place the peanut butter in a saucepan and cook over medium heat, stirring all the time, until runny, or place in a microwavable pitcher or bowl and heat on medium in the microwave for around 20 seconds, or until runny (see Tips).

❷ Add the yogurt to the peanut butter and stir well to combine, then add the chicken strips and stir to coat with the dressing.

❸ Spoon the chicken mixture onto 2 slices of the bread, then top with the remaining bread (see Tips). Serve with strips of cucumber and some crunchy salad greens.

⭐ *Tips: Softening times for the peanut butter vary according to microwave wattage, as follows: 800W—10 seconds; 750W—20 seconds; 650W— 30 seconds. You don't need butter or spread on the bread, as the peanut butter dressing serves the same purpose.*

Whole grain per serving **2**   Prep time **5 mins**

tuna pita pockets

7 oz/200 g canned tuna in water or oil, very well drained
  (see Tip)
2 tomatoes, coarsely chopped
3½ oz/100 g canned cannellini beans, drained and rinsed
2 tbsp olive oil
2 whole wheat pitas
salt and pepper
salad greens, to serve

❶ Tip the tuna into a bowl and break it up into bite-size
chunks with a fork.

❷ Add the tomatoes to the bowl with the cannellini beans
and oil. Season with a little salt and pepper and stir gently
to combine.

❸ Using a sharp knife, cut the pitas in half horizontally, then
split to form pockets and stuff the tuna mixture inside. Serve
with salad greens.

⭐ *Tip: Try not to use tuna in brine, as it is very high in salt.*

Whole grain
per serving
2

Prep time
5 mins

italian chicken wraps

3 tbsp lowfat mayonnaise
1½ tbsp store-bought red pesto
5½ oz/150 g cooked chicken breast fillet, plain or flavored,
  cut into strips (see Tip)
2 whole wheat or corn tortillas
salad greens, to serve

❶ Mix together the mayonnaise and pesto in a bowl, then tip in the chicken strips and stir well.

❷ Lay the tortillas out flat and place half the chicken mix in the center of each, then roll up to form a wrap. Serve with salad greens.

⭐ Tip: You can use cooked, store-bought chicken breast fillet, which comes in several flavors, such as barbecue.

Whole grain per serving 1   Serves 2   Prep. time 5 mins

grilled chicken baguette

2 thick slices whole wheat baguette (see Tip)
4 tsp lowfat spread
2 tbsp reduced-fat mayonnaise
1 tsp store-bought red pesto
3½ oz/100 g cooked chicken breast pieces,
   grilled or barbecued
2 large scallions, finely chopped
2 ripe tomatoes
2–3 crisp lettuce leaves, sliced

❶ Split the baguette in half and spread the cut surfaces with the lowfat spread.

❷ Beat the mayonnaise with the pesto in a small bowl until well combined, then stir in the chicken pieces and scallions until well coated.

❸ Slice the tomatoes onto the baguette, then top with the chicken mixture and lettuce. Close the sandwich, cut into 2 pieces, and serve.

⭐ Tip: You can use any crusty, robust, country-style, whole wheat bread for this delicious sandwich.

Whole grain
per serving
2

Prep. time
5mins

lemony mini dip pots

juice of ½ lemon
5½ oz/150 g reduced-fat hummus
1 tbsp olive oil
2 carrots (see Tip)
2 whole wheat pitas

❶ Stir the lemon juice into the hummus with the oil and divide between 2 small pots.

❷ Cut the carrots into thick sticks.

❸ Toast the pitas and cut into strips, then serve the hummus dip with the carrots and pita strips.

⭐ *Tip: Try other raw vegetables in place of the carrots, or make yourself a selection—red bell pepper slices, scallions, and celery are all ideal.*

Whole grain per serving 2 | Serves 2 | Prep time 8 mins

savory lunchbox energy bars

1 egg
heaping ½ cup grated sharp cheddar cheese
scant 1 cup rolled oats
2 tbsp butter, softened

❶ Preheat the oven to 375°F/190°C. Meanwhile, beat the egg.

❷ Using a fork, mix together the egg, cheese, oats, and butter in a bowl until thoroughly combined.

❸ Press the mixture evenly into a shallow 7 x 4-inch/18 x 10-cm cake pan and bake in the preheated oven for 25 minutes, until golden. Let cool, then cut into quarters.

Whole grain per bar
1

Prep. time
35mins

quick pita pizzas

2 whole wheat pita breads
5 tbsp store-bought tomato sauce for pizza
3½ oz/100 g canned tuna in water or oil, drained (see Tips)
heaping 3 tbsp corn kernels
3½ oz/100 g mozzarella cheese, thinly sliced

❶ Preheat the broiler, lightly sprinkle the pita breads with water, and toast one side until piping hot and springy to the touch.

❷ Remove the broiler pan from the broiler, turn the pitas, and spread them evenly with the tomato sauce, followed by the tuna and corn (see Tips) and, finally, the cheese slices.

❸ Return to the broiler and cook until the cheese is bubbling and melted. Serve immediately.

⭐ *Tips: Try not to use tuna in brine, as it is very high in salt. Instead of tuna and corn, you can make a topping of thinly sliced button mushrooms and ham or leftover cooked chicken breast.*

Whole grain per serving **2**   Prep. time **10** mins

stir-fried cheesy tomatoes on toast

2 tbsp light olive oil
1 lb/450 g ripe tomatoes, coarsely chopped (see Tips)
2 scallions, chopped
2 tsp Worcestershire sauce
heaping 2 cups grated sharp cheddar or mozzarella cheese
  (see Tips)
2 slices whole wheat bread

❶ Heat the oil in a nonstick skillet and stir-fry the tomatoes over medium–high heat for 5–7 minutes, until they begin to soften. Add the scallions and Worcestershire sauce and stir for an additional 2 minutes. Stir in three-quarters of the cheese. Meanwhile, toast the bread.

❷ When the toast is ready, pile the tomato mixture on top and serve sprinkled with the remaining grated cheese.

⭐ *Tips: Try to buy ripe, flavorsome tomatoes for this dish. If using mozzarella, buy the hard type in a block or use pregrated cheese.*

Whole grain per serving

1

Prep. time

9 mins

scrambled eggs deluxe

4 large eggs
3 tbsp skim or lowfat milk
2 tbsp lowfat spread
3½ oz/100 g smoked salmon pieces
2 slices whole wheat bread (see Tip)
salt and pepper
finely chopped fresh parsley, to garnish

❶ Break the eggs into a bowl, add the milk and salt and pepper to taste, and beat to combine. Melt three-quarters of the lowfat spread in a nonstick saucepan, add the egg mixture, and cook over low–medium heat, occasionally stirring gently, until just beginning to set.

❷ Add the smoked salmon pieces and stir gently to mix.

❸ Meanwhile, toast the bread, then spread with the remaining lowfat spread.

❹ When the eggs are scrambled to your liking, pile them on the toast and garnish with parsley to serve.

⭐ *Tip: The egg and salmon topping is also delicious served on or with sliced dark rye bread, which can be bought from most supermarkets. This would raise the number of whole grain servings per portion to 1.5.*

Whole grain per serving	Serves	Prep. time
1	2	8 mins

herby pasta and vegetable soup

2 tbsp sunflower, light olive, or vegetable oil
1 large onion, finely chopped (see Tips)
2 carrots, finely chopped (see Tips)
14 oz/400 g canned chopped tomatoes with herbs
1 cup frozen green beans
3 cups vegetable stock
4½ oz/125 g whole wheat fusilli pasta
salt and pepper
fresh flat-leaf parsley, to garnish

❶ Heat the oil in a large saucepan, then add the onion and carrots.

❷ Cook over medium heat, stirring occasionally, for about 6–7 minutes, until softened.

❸ Add the tomatoes, green beans, stock, and pasta, stir well, and bring to a simmer. Cook, stirring occasionally, for around 20 minutes, or until the pasta and vegetables are tender. Check the seasoning, adding salt and pepper to taste, and garnish with fresh parsley (see Tips).

★ *Tips: You can use 1 large leek instead of the onion, and butternut squash instead of the carrots, if you like. You can also garnish the soup with grated cheese.*

Whole grain per serving | | Prep. time
1 | | 30 mins

fast tomato pasta

4½ oz/125 g whole wheat fusilli pasta
½ tsp salt
3–4 ripe tomatoes, coarsely chopped
1 heaping tbsp sun-dried tomatoes in oil, drained and finely
   chopped, plus 1½ tbsp of the oil from the jar
2 tbsp toasted pine nuts
handful of fresh basil leaves

❶ Cook the pasta in a large saucepan of boiling, lightly salted
water for about 12 minutes, until just tender, then drain.

❷ Toss the cooked pasta with the tomatoes, sun-dried
tomatoes, oil, pine nuts, and basil leaves in a large bowl.
Spoon into serving dishes.

Whole grain per serving	Serves	Prep. time
2	2	10 mins

spanish sausage pasta

3½ oz/100 g whole wheat penne pasta
½ tsp salt
generous ⅓ cup olive oil
1 onion, coarsely chopped
1 red bell pepper, seeded and coarsely chopped
1 green bell pepper, seeded and coarsely chopped
3½ oz/100 g chorizo sausage, sliced (see Tip)
2 tsp balsamic vinegar
1 tbsp red wine vinegar
1 tbsp sweet chili dipping sauce

❶ Cook the pasta in a large saucepan of boiling, lightly salted water for about 10 minutes, until just tender.

❷ Heat 2 tablespoons of the oil in a large, nonstick skillet and stir-fry the onion and bell peppers over medium–high heat for 5 minutes, or until softened and the onions are turning golden. Add the chorizo to the skillet and cook for an additional 5 minutes.

❸ Mix the remaining oil, both vinegars, and chili sauce in a serving bowl to make a dressing. Drain the pasta and toss with the vegetable mixture and dressing.

⭐ *Tip: Chorizo is a spicy Spanish sausage available in vacuum packs in supermarket cooked meat cabinets. For a milder sausage, use pepperoni.*

Whole grain per serving		Prep time
1.5		20 mins

cheese and tomato pasta salad

4½ oz/125 g whole wheat fusilli pasta
½ tsp salt
4½ oz/125 g sharp cheddar cheese, cubed
12 small or 6 large cherry tomatoes, halved (see Tips)
4 tbsp store-bought Italian dressing (see Tips)

❶ Cook the pasta in boiling, lightly salted water for about 12 minutes, until just tender, then drain well and let cool.

❷ Mix together the cooled pasta, cheese, tomatoes, and dressing and serve as a salad (see Tips).

⭐ *Tips: You can also substitute some, or all, of the cherry tomatoes with sun-dried tomatoes in oil or chopped tomatoes. Bottles of store-bought Italian dressing are readily available in supermarkets. This is a tasty basic salad—you can experiment and try adding flavorings, such as chopped parsley or scallions or a little finely chopped fresh mild chile.*

Whole grain per serving	Serves	Prep. time
2	2	20mins

three bean salad

½ cup (dry weight) brown rice
½ tsp salt
3½ oz/100 g trimmed green beans, halved
4 tbsp store-bought Italian dressing
2 tbsp strained tomatoes
1 large or 2 medium tomatoes, seeded and chopped
7 oz/200 g canned red kidney beans, drained and rinsed
7 oz/200 g canned cannellini or lima beans, drained
  and rinsed

❶ Cook the rice in boiling, lightly salted water until tender, drain if necessary, and let cool.

❷ Cook the green beans, uncovered, in a small saucepan of boiling water for about 3 minutes, until just softened but still slightly firm to the bite. Drain and let cool.

❸ While the beans and rice are cooking, mix together the dressing, strained tomatoes, and chopped tomato in a bowl and stir in the kidney and cannellini beans. Add the cooled green beans and rice and stir through before spooning into serving bowls.

Whole grain per serving 1.5 | Serves 2 | Prep time 30 mins

spicy rice with shrimp and eggs

2 eggs
½ cup (dry weight) brown rice
½ tsp salt
2 tbsp sesame or sunflower oil
5½-oz/150-g package stir-fry vegetables
2 tsp ready-chopped garlic (see Tips)
2 tsp ready-chopped ginger (see Tips)
1 tbsp light soy sauce
3½ oz/100 g peeled cooked shrimp

❶ Cook the eggs in a saucepan of boiling water for 8 minutes, until just hard-boiled. Cook the rice in boiling, lightly salted water until tender, drain if necessary, and let cool.

❷ Heat the oil in a nonstick skillet and stir-fry the vegetables for 2–3 minutes, adding the garlic, ginger, soy sauce, and shrimp for the last minute.

❸ Shell and quarter the eggs. Stir the rice into the vegetable mixture, then divide between 2 serving bowls and top with the egg quarters.

⭐ *Tips: Small jars of finely chopped garlic and ginger are widely available at supermarkets, but if you prefer, you can use finely chopped fresh garlic and ginger.*

Whole grain per serving	Serves	Prep time
1.5	2	25mins

veggie rice salad

½ cup (dry weight) brown rice
½ tsp salt
3 tbsp olive oil
juice of ½ small lemon
2 large tomatoes, seeded and coarsely chopped
1 small red onion, finely chopped
½ red bell pepper, broiled and chopped (see Tip)
generous handful chopped fresh parsley and mint
  or chopped fresh cilantro
⅓ cup toasted pine nuts
salt and pepper

❶ Cook the rice in boiling, lightly salted water until tender, drain if necessary, and let cool.

❷ Mix together the oil and lemon juice and season to taste with salt and pepper.

❸ Add the tomatoes, onion, bell pepper, most of the herbs, the pine nuts, and the oil and lemon juice mixture to the rice and stir thoroughly. Serve immediately garnished with the remaining herbs.

⭐ *Tip: You can buy broiled or roasted red bell peppers preserved in water, brine, or oil in jars or cans at the supermarket. Leftover bell peppers will keep for a week in their oil or brine in an airtight container in the refrigerator.*

Whole grain
per serving
1.5

fruity rice salad

½ cup (dry weight) brown rice
½ tsp salt
2 tbsp light olive oil
1½ tsp orange juice
1 red apple, cored and chopped (see Tip)
6 plumped dried apricots, chopped
3¼-inch/8-cm piece of cucumber, chopped
2 tbsp toasted slivered almonds
salt and pepper

❶ Cook the rice in boiling, lightly salted water until tender, drain if necessary, and let cool.

❷ Meanwhile, beat together the oil and orange juice in a bowl and add salt and pepper to taste.

❸ Add the apple, apricots, cucumber, almonds, and the oil and orange juice mixture to the rice and stir thoroughly. Serve immediately.

⭐ *Tip: If you like, peel and chop an orange and add to the salad or use instead of the apple.*

Whole grain per serving	Serves	Prep Time
1.5	2	30mins

delicious
dinners

world's best burger

2½ tbsp light olive oil
1 large mild onion, thinly sliced
14 oz/400 g lean ground beef
1 egg, beaten
2 tsp dried mixed herbs
4 large whole wheat buns
2 tomatoes, sliced
salt and pepper
salad greens, to serve

❶ Heat 2 tablespoons of the oil in a large, nonstick skillet. Add the onion to the pan and cook over medium–high heat, stirring occasionally, for 8–10 minutes, until golden and softened.

❷ Mix together the ground beef, egg, and herbs in a bowl and add salt and pepper to taste. Form into 4 round, flat patties. Brush the bottom of another nonstick pan with the remaining oil and place over high heat. Add the burgers and cook for 3 minutes, then turn over and cook for an additional 2 minutes, until cooked through.

❸ Split the buns and place the sliced tomatoes on the bottom halves. Put the burgers on top of the tomatoes and then add the cooked onions. Serve with salad greens.

Whole grain per serving | serves | Prep time
2 | 4 | 10 mins

chili con carne

1½ cups (dry weight) brown rice
½ tsp salt
2 tbsp sunflower, light olive, or vegetable oil
1 large onion, finely chopped
2 green bell peppers, seeded and chopped
1 lb 2 oz/500 g lean ground beef
3 tsp ready-chopped chile, or to taste
2 tsp ready-chopped garlic, or to taste
generous 2 cups store-bought tomato sauce for pasta
7 oz/200 g canned red kidney beans, drained and rinsed
1 tbsp plain yogurt
fresh flat-leaf parsley, to garnish
salad greens, to serve

❶ Cook the rice in boiling, lightly salted water until tender and drain if necessary.

❷ Meanwhile, heat the oil in a large, nonstick skillet and stir-fry the onion and bell peppers over medium–high heat for about 5 minutes, until soft, then add the beef and cook, stirring, until browned. Add the chile and garlic and cook for an additional minute.

❸ Stir in the tomato sauce and kidney beans, bring to a simmer, cover, and cook for 15–20 minutes (longer if you have the time). Serve the meat sauce with the rice, top with some plain yogurt, and garnish with parsley. Serve with salad greens.

Whole grain
per serving
2.5

spaghetti with mini meatballs

10½ oz/300 g whole wheat spaghetti
½ tsp salt
1 small mild onion, finely chopped
1 lb/450 g lean ground beef
1 egg, beaten
2 tbsp light olive oil
1¾ cups store-bought tomato sauce for pasta
salt and pepper
fresh basil sprigs, to garnish

❶ Cook the spaghetti in a large saucepan of boiling, lightly salted water for about 10 minutes, until just tender.

❷ Meanwhile, put the onion in a bowl. Add the ground beef and egg, season to taste with salt and pepper, and stir well to combine (see Tip). Using your hands, form the mixture into 28–32 small balls. Meanwhile, heat the oil in a nonstick skillet.

❸ Add the meatballs to the skillet and cook over medium–high heat, turning once or twice, for 3 minutes, until browned. Spoon off and discard the surplus fat. Add the pasta sauce, bring to a simmer, and cook for an additional 2–3 minutes, until the meatballs are cooked through. Drain the spaghetti and serve with the meatballs and sauce, garnished with basil.

⭐ *Tip: Add some paprika or mixed herbs to the meatball mixture.*

Whole grain per serving	Serves	Prep: time
2.5	4	20 mins

curried pork kebabs with rice

1¼ cups plain yogurt
1 tbsp mild curry paste, or to taste (see Tips)
1 lb 5 oz/600 g lean pork tenderloin, cubed (see Tips)
1½ cups (dry weight) brown rice
½ tsp salt
salad greens with herbs, to serve

❶ Beat the yogurt and curry paste together in a large bowl. Add the pork, cover, and let marinate for up to 1 hour.

❷ Cook the rice in boiling, lightly salted water until tender and drain if necessary.

❸ Meanwhile, preheat the broiler and thread the pork onto 4 metal kebab skewers. Broil on medium–high heat, turning 2–3 times, for about 12 minutes, until the pork is cooked through and no traces of pink remain. Serve the kebabs with the cooked rice and salad greens with herbs.

⭐ *Tips: Try substituting a Chinese stir-fry sauce, such as hoisin, for the curry paste. You can also use chicken or lamb fillet for this recipe.*

Whole grain per serving
2.5

Prep time
25 mins

ham and pineapple pizza

12 oz/350 g whole wheat bread mix
generous 1 cup warm water
1½ tbsp olive or vegetable oil, plus extra for oiling and
   brushing
all-purpose flour, for dusting
1¼ cups store-bought tomato pizza or pasta sauce
7 oz/200 g canned pineapple pieces in juice, drained
5½ oz/150 g wafer-thin ham, broken into pieces
3½ oz/100 g soft mozzarella cheese, thinly sliced

❶ Make a dough with the bread mix, water, and oil and
knead for 10 minutes, or according to the package directions.
Shape the dough into a ball, put it into an oiled bowl, cover,
and let stand in a warm place for 30–40 minutes, until risen.
Meanwhile, preheat the oven to 400°F/200°C and lightly brush a
12-inch/30-cm pizza pan with oil.

❷ Roll out the dough on a floured counter to a 12-inch/
30-cm circle, then lift it onto the prepared pizza pan.

❸ Top the pizza first with a thin layer of tomato sauce (you
may not need all of it), then with the pineapple and ham
and, finally, with the cheese slices, leaving a ¾-inch/2-cm
margin around the edge. Bake in the preheated oven for
15–20 minutes, until the edge of the crust is crisp and golden
and the cheese is bubbling.

Whole grain
per serving
4

Prep time
75mins

creamy mushroom and bacon pasta

10½ oz/300 g whole wheat tagliatelle or spaghetti
½ tsp salt
2 tbsp olive oil
7 oz/200 g lean unsmoked Canadian bacon, chopped
10½ oz/300 g cremini mushrooms, sliced
generous ¾ cup reduced-fat sour cream
salt and pepper

❶ Cook the pasta in a large saucepan of boiling, lightly salted water for 10–12 minutes, until just tender.

❷ Heat the oil in a large, nonstick skillet, add the bacon and mushrooms, and stir-fry until the bacon is becoming crisp and the mushrooms are cooked through.

❸ Add the sour cream and heat through, stirring. Taste and add a little salt, if necessary, and some pepper.

❹ When the pasta is cooked, drain and toss with the sauce in a large, warmed serving bowl.

Whole grain
per serving
2.5

chicken nuggets

4 slices day-old whole wheat bread, crusts removed
2 eggs
4 tbsp whole wheat flour
4 skinless chicken breast fillets, cubed
sunflower oil, for shallow-frying
mixed side salad, to serve

❶ Tear the bread into pieces and process in a blender for a few seconds to make crumbs. Beat the eggs in a shallow dish.

❷ Put the flour and breadcrumbs into separate shallow dishes. Dip each chicken cube first in the flour, then in the beaten eggs and, finally, in the breadcrumbs until thoroughly coated.

❸ Heat a little sunflower oil in a large, nonstick skillet and cook the nuggets over medium–high heat, turning to cook all sides, for 8 minutes, or until cooked through and golden (see Tip). Serve with a mixed side salad.

⭐ *Tip: Test one nugget by cutting through to the center—if any pink remains, cook for a little longer. If you prefer, you can cut the chicken into strips to produce fingers rather than nuggets. You can also bake the nuggets rather than pan-fry them—spray them thoroughly with cooking oil spray and bake in a preheated oven at 350°F/180°C for 15–20 minutes.*

Whole grain
per serving
2

Prep time
20mins

asian express chicken

½ cup (dry weight) brown rice
½ tsp salt
½ cup frozen peas
2 tbsp sunflower or light olive oil
4 large scallions, trimmed and sliced diagonally
2 tsp Chinese spice mix
1 tbsp water
2 cooked skinless, boneless chicken breasts or legs,
  cut into strips
2 eggs, beaten
1 tbsp light soy sauce

❶ Cook the rice in boiling, lightly salted water until tender, drain if necessary, and set aside.

❷ Cook the peas in a small saucepan of water for 4 minutes, until cooked through, then drain and let cool slightly.

❸ Heat the oil in a nonstick skillet, add the scallions and spice mix, and stir-fry over medium heat for 1 minute. Add the rice and the water and stir-fry, breaking up any lumps of rice.

❹ Add the chicken and peas and stir for 1 minute, then move the mixture to the side of the skillet. Add the eggs, increase the heat to medium–high, and cook for 1 minute. Stir the eggs into the rice, then stir in the soy sauce. Serve in warmed bowls.

Whole grain
per serving
1.5

chicken chow mein

3½ oz/100 g whole wheat ribbon noodles
2 tbsp sesame or vegetable oil
10½ oz/300 g skinless chicken breast fillets, cut into strips
1 zucchini, thinly sliced
1 carrot, thinly sliced
1 red bell pepper, seeded and thinly sliced
1¾ oz/50 g snow peas or peas
4 large scallions, thinly sliced
2 tsp Chinese spice mix
1 tbsp light soy sauce
1 tbsp oyster sauce
3–4 tbsp chicken stock

❶ Cook the noodles in a saucepan of boiling water for
2–3 minutes or according to the package directions, until
just tender but still with some bite.

❷ Heat the oil in a wok or nonstick skillet and stir-fry the
chicken and zucchini, carrot, bell pepper, snow peas, and
scallions over high heat for 5 minutes, until the chicken is
cooked through and the vegetables are tender.

❸ Add the Chinese spice, soy sauce, oyster sauce,
and chicken stock and stir for an additional minute. Drain
the noodles, add to the pan, and stir again for 1 minute
before serving.

Whole grain per serving
1.5

Prep time
20 mins

fantastic fish sticks

4 slices day-old whole wheat bread, crusts removed
3 tbsp all-purpose flour
2 eggs, beaten
1 lb 9 oz/700 g firm whitefish fillets
2 tbsp sunflower or light olive oil
fresh flat-leaf parsley, to garnish
cooked green vegetables and ketchup, to serve

❶ Coarsely break up the bread and process in a blender to make crumbs. Put the flour, eggs, and breadcrumbs into three separate shallow, wide dishes. Using a sharp knife, cut the fish into 16–20 sticks.

❷ Dip each fish stick first in the flour to coat all over, then in the eggs and, finally, coat thoroughly with the breadcrumbs.

❸ Heat the oil in a large, nonstick skillet (you may have to use two). Cook the fish sticks over medium–high heat for about 3 minutes, until the undersides are golden, then turn over and cook for an additional 2 minutes. Check that the fish is cooked through before serving, garnished with parsley. Serve with a portion of green vegetables and ketchup.

⭐ *Tip: You can use salmon to make fish sticks rich in omega-3.*

Whole grain per serving
1

Prep. time
10 mins

tuna noodle casserole

10½ oz/300 g whole wheat pasta shapes
½ tsp salt
2 tbsp olive or vegetable oil
1 large onion, chopped
1 large green bell pepper, seeded and chopped
1 large garlic clove, chopped
14 oz/400 g canned chopped tomatoes with herbs
1 tbsp tomato paste
14 oz/400 g canned tuna, well drained
heaping 1 cup grated cheddar cheese
4 tbsp whole wheat breadcrumbs
fresh flat-leaf parsley, to garnish

❶ Preheat the oven to 375°F/190°C. Cook the pasta in a saucepan of boiling, lightly salted water for 12 minutes, until just tender, then drain.

❷ Heat the oil in a large, nonstick skillet and stir-fry the onion and bell pepper over medium–high heat for 8 minutes, until softened. Add the garlic and stir for an additional minute.

❸ Add the tomatoes, tomato paste, tuna, and drained pasta and warm through, then transfer to a shallow, ovenproof dish, spread out evenly, and sprinkle with the cheese and breadcrumbs. Bake in the preheated oven for 25 minutes, until the top is golden. Garnish with parsley.

Whole grain per serving **3**

Prep. time **40** mins

sticky salmon with noodles

14 oz/400 g salmon fillet, skinned and cut into chunks
2 tbsp teriyaki marinade, plus extra to serve
7 oz/200 g whole wheat ribbon noodles
1 small head of broccoli (see Tips)
1 tbsp olive oil

❶ Place the salmon into a bowl, add the teriyaki marinade, and mix gently (see Tips).

❷ Cook the noodles in a large pan of boiling water for about 2–3 minutes or according to the package directions. Meanwhile, cut the broccoli into small florets and steam over a saucepan of boiling water, or cook in the microwave for about 3 minutes with 1 tablespoon of water, until just tender (see Tips).

❸ Drain the noodles and tip into a warmed serving bowl. Heat the oil in a skillet and stir-fry the salmon pieces over high heat for 2–3 minutes, until just cooked through. Toss the salmon with the noodles and broccoli and drizzle with a little extra teriyaki marinade, to serve.

⭐ *Tips: You could use snow peas instead of the broccoli. If you have time, cover the bowl of salmon and let marinate for up to 1 hour. Cooking times for the broccoli vary according to microwave wattage, as follows: 800W—2.5 minutes; 750W—3 minutes; 650W—3.5 minutes.*

Whole grain per serving	Serves	Prep time
1.5	4	10 mins

seafood creole

2 tbsp sunflower or light olive oil
1 large green bell pepper, seeded and cut into chunks
scant 1 cup corn kernels
1 cup (dry weight) brown rice
2½ cups vegetable stock
14 oz/400 g firm whitefish or salmon fillet, in chunks
8 oz/225 g cooked peeled shrimp
1¾ cups store-bought tomato, chile, and bell pepper sauce
  for pasta
chili powder, to garnish
fresh flat-leaf parsley, to garnish

❶ Heat the oil in a large, nonstick skillet. Stir-fry the bell pepper over medium–high heat for about 3 minutes, until it softens. Add the corn and stir for an additional minute.

❷ Meanwhile, cook the rice, covered, in the stock until tender, by which time all the stock should be absorbed, and add to the skillet, stirring well.

❸ Add the fish, shrimp, and sauce to the pan, stir gently to combine, and simmer for 3–4 minutes, or until the fish is cooked through. Sprinkle lightly with chili powder and add parsley to garnish. Serve immediately.

Whole grain per serving 1.5   Prep. time 30 mins

creamy mushroom crêpes

4 tbsp light olive oil
9 oz/250 g cremini mushrooms, sliced
1 tsp dried thyme or 2 tsp fresh thyme leaves
2 tbsp chopped fresh flat-leaf parsley
generous ¾ cup reduced-fat sour cream
½ cup whole wheat flour
½ tsp baking powder
¼ tsp salt
1 egg
generous ¾ cup lowfat or skim milk
salt and pepper

❶ Heat 2 tablespoons of the oil in a saucepan. Add the mushrooms, thyme, and half the parsley. Season to taste with salt and pepper and cook over high heat for 2 minutes. Stir in the sour cream.

❷ Sieve together the flour, baking powder, and salt into a bowl, then beat in the egg and milk, and add salt and pepper to taste. Heat ½ tablespoon of the remaining oil in a 8-inch/20-cm nonstick skillet until very hot. Add a quarter of the batter, tilting the pan to cover the bottom. Cook over high heat for 30 seconds, then flip the crêpe over and cook for an additional minute. Slide it on to a warmed plate. Repeat to make 3 more crêpes.

❸ Spoon a quarter of the mushroom mixture into the center of each crêpe and fold over. Sprinkle with the remaining parsley.

Whole grain per serving	Serves	Prep time
2	2	10 mins

spaghetti napolitana

10½ oz/300 g whole wheat spaghetti
½ tsp salt
2 tbsp light olive oil
1 large onion, chopped
2 garlic cloves, chopped
1 lb 12 oz/800 g canned chopped tomatoes
1 tbsp tomato paste
1 tsp superfine sugar
2 tbsp grated Parmesan cheese
salt and pepper
fresh basil, to garnish

❶ Cook the spaghetti in a large saucepan of boiling, lightly salted water for about 10 minutes, until just tender, then drain.

❷ Meanwhile, heat the oil in a large, nonstick skillet and cook the onion and garlic over medium–high heat, stirring frequently, for about 5 minutes, until soft and transparent.

❸ Add the tomatoes, tomato paste, sugar, and salt and pepper to taste, stir, and cook gently for 15 minutes, until thickened and rich (see Tip). Check the seasoning before mixing the sauce with the spaghetti. Top with the cheese. Garnish with basil to serve.

⭐ *Tip: You can add some chili sauce or fresh basil to the tomato sauce for a change.*

Whole grain per serving
2.5

Prep time
20 mins

cheesy pasta gratin

3 tbsp butter
1 heaping tbsp all-purpose flour
generous 2½ cups lowfat or skim milk
scant 1 cup grated cheddar cheese
10½ oz/300 g whole wheat penne pasta
½ tsp salt
1 small head of broccoli
3 tomatoes, quartered
4 tbsp whole wheat breadcrumbs
salt and pepper

❶ Melt the butter in a nonstick saucepan, add the flour, and stir over medium heat to combine well, then gradually stir in the milk and bring to a simmer. Stir until smooth, then add two-thirds of the cheese and season to taste with salt and pepper.

❷ Meanwhile, preheat the oven to 375°F/190°C. Cook the pasta in a saucepan of boiling, lightly salted water for about 12 minutes, until just tender, then drain and tip into an ovenproof dish. Put the broccoli and tomatoes on top and pour over the cheese sauce.

❸ Top with the remaining cheese and the breadcrumbs and bake in the preheated oven for about 25 minutes, until the topping is golden and bubbling.

Whole grain per serving
3

taste of italy pasta

10½ oz/300 g whole wheat penne pasta
½ tsp salt
4½ oz/125 g store-bought green pesto
3–4 tbsp olive oil
24 cherry tomatoes, halved
scant 1 cup grated Parmesan cheese

❶ Cook the pasta in a large saucepan of lightly salted, boiling water for about 12 minutes, until just cooked.

❷ Meanwhile, beat the pesto in a bowl with enough of the oil to make a dressing the consistency of heavy cream (an electric hand whisk will do the job very well).

❸ Add the tomatoes and two-thirds of the cheese to the dressing.

❹ When the pasta is cooked, drain well and transfer to a large serving bowl. Tip in the dressing mixture and stir well. Serve with the remaining cheese sprinkled on top.

Whole grain per serving 2.5   Serves   Prep. time 15mins

super-quick veggie pizza

14 oz/400 g whole wheat bread mix
1 tbsp olive oil, plus extra for oiling and brushing
2 large red bell peppers, seeded and chopped
all-purpose flour, for dusting
1¼ cups store-bought tomato and red bell pepper pasta sauce
7 oz/200 g soft mozzarella, sliced
mixed salad greens, to serve

❶ Make up the bread mix according to the package directions and knead for 5 minutes. Shape the dough into a ball and put it into an oiled bowl. Cover and let stand in a warm place for 30 minutes, until risen.

❷ Preheat the oven to 400°F/200°C and lightly oil a pizza pan. Heat the oil in a skillet and stir-fry the bell peppers for 1–2 minutes, until slightly softened.

❸ Roll out the dough on a floured counter to a 12-inch/ 30-cm circle and lift it onto the prepared pan. Top the pizza first with the pasta sauce (you may not need all of it), then with the peppers and, finally, with the mozzarella. Bake in the preheated oven for 15 minutes, until the topping is bubbling and golden. Serve with mixed salad greens.

Whole grain per serving	Serves	Prep. time
5	4	1 hour

dreamy
desserts

peach and raspberry crunch sundae

4 slices whole wheat bread, crusts removed
3–4 tbsp sunflower oil
2 large ripe peaches
scant 1 cup raspberries
1 tbsp confectioners' sugar
4 scoops vanilla ice cream
¼ cup store-bought berry sauce (see Tip)

❶ Coarsely break up the bread, then process in a blender to make crumbs and tip into a bowl. Stir in the oil to coat all the bread thoroughly, then tip into a large, nonstick skillet and cook over medium–high heat, stirring occasionally, for about 3 minutes, until the breadcrumbs are crisp. Watch carefully to prevent scorching. Remove the crumbs from the skillet and let cool for 1–2 minutes.

❷ Meanwhile, pit and slice the peaches and put them into a bowl with the raspberries and confectioners' sugar. Stir until the sugar has dissolved.

❸ Arrange the fruit mixture, ice cream, and breadcrumbs in sundae glasses and top each with a drizzle of sauce. Serve immediately.

⭐ *Tip: You can buy bottles of berry sauce in the supermarket—they are often labeled "coulis."*

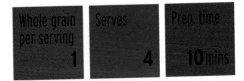

Whole grain per serving	Serves	Prep. time
1	4	10 mins

berry crunch

3¼ cups raspberries
¾ cup blueberries
2 tbsp sugar
2 tbsp water
4 slices whole wheat bread (see Tips)
2 tbsp peanut or sunflower oil
generous ¾ cup light cream (see Tips)

❶ Put the berries in a saucepan with the sugar and water.
Bring to a simmer and cook gently for 5–10 minutes, until
you have a richly colored juice but the berries are still whole.

❷ Meanwhile, remove the crusts from the bread and cut each
slice into 2 triangles. Heat the oil in a large, nonstick skillet
and pan-fry the bread on both sides over high heat until
lightly golden.

❸ Put the bread onto 4 serving plates. Divide the berry
mixture equally among them, covering about half of each
bread triangle. Pour over the cream and serve.

⭐ *Tips: For a lighter option, use toasted bread instead of pan-fried bread.*
You can serve this dessert with vanilla ice cream or thick yogurt instead of the
light cream, if you like.

Whole grain
per serving
1

Prep. time
20 mins

apple toastie

2 small sweet red apples, cored and thinly sliced
4 tbsp golden raisins
1 tbsp honey
1 tsp pumpkin pie spice
juice of ½ lemon
2 tbsp lowfat spread
4 slices whole wheat bread

❶ Place the apple slices, raisins, honey, pumpkin pie spice, and lemon juice in a saucepan with half of the lowfat spread and cook over medium heat, stirring constantly, for about 8 minutes, until the apples have softened.

❷ Toast the bread, spread with the remaining lowfat spread, and top with the apple mixture (see Tip).

Tip: If you have a sandwich toaster, spread 8 bread slices with lowfat spread. Mix the sliced apples with the golden raisins, honey, pumpkin pie spice, and lemon juice. Use the bread and apple filling to make toasted sandwiches in the sandwich toaster according to the manufacturer's instructions. This increases the recipe to 2 whole grain portions.

Whole grain per serving	Serves	Prep. time
1	4	10 mins

strawberry scones

4 whole wheat scones
1⅓ cups strawberries, hulled and sliced (see Tip)
generous ¾ cup plain strained yogurt
2 tsp superfine sugar
4 tbsp store-bought strawberry sauce (coulis)

❶ Preheat the broiler. Slice each scone into three layers and toast the slices under the broiler.

❷ Meanwhile, mix half the strawberries with the yogurt and sugar.

❸ Place the toasted scones on plates and spoon the strawberry mixture between the slices and on top. Decorate the scones with the remaining strawberries and drizzle with the strawberry sauce. Serve immediately.

⭐ *Tip: You can adapt the recipe using any other seasonal berries.*

Whole grain per serving **2** | Serves **4** | Prep. time **5 mins**

honeyed plums

3 tbsp honey
2 tbsp butter
6 ripe red-skinned plums, pitted and halved
4 slices whole wheat bread

❶ Mix together the honey and butter in a small saucepan or microwavable bowl. Cover and cook over medium–high heat, stirring constantly, until the honey and butter have melted, or cover and cook in the microwave for 1 minute (see Tip).

❷ Meanwhile, preheat the broiler. Arrange the plums closely together, with cut side up, in a single layer in a shallow ovenproof dish.

❸ When the honey sauce is ready, spoon it over the plums and place the dish under the hot broiler for 7 minutes, or until the plums are tender when pierced with the point of a sharp knife. Meanwhile, toast the bread.

❹ Serve the plum halves on the toast and spoon all the sauce over them.

⭐ *Tip: Cooking times for the honey and butter vary according to microwave wattage, as follows: 800W—0.5 minutes; 750W—1 minute; 650W—1.5 minutes.*

Whole grain per serving	Serves	Prep. time
1	4	10 mins

sweet peach delight

4½ tbsp butter
scant 1 cup whole wheat flour
1½ tsp baking powder
¼ tsp salt
¾ cup lowfat or skim milk
scant ¾ cup sugar
4 large ripe peaches, pitted, peeled, and sliced (see Tip)

❶ Preheat the oven to 350°F/180°C. Melt the butter in
a saucepan over low heat and pour it into the bottom
of a shallow 8-inch/20-cm square ovenproof dish.

❷ Sieve the flour, baking powder and salt into a mixing bowl
and blend in the milk and sugar, then pour the mixture into the
dish. Spoon the peach slices over the batter but do not stir.
Bake in the preheated oven for 50 minutes.

⭐ Tip: You can use other seasonal fruit for this dish, such as plums
or pears. You could also use good-quality, drained, canned fruits.

Whole grain
per serving
2

Prep. time
70 mins

mixed berry crumble

1 lb 2 oz/500 g mixed berries (see Tip)
scant ½ cup sugar
scant 1 cup whole wheat flour
4½ tbsp butter
2 tbsp chopped mixed nuts

❶ Combine the berries with 3 tablespoons of the sugar in an ovenproof dish. Preheat the oven to 350°F/180°C.

❷ Put the flour into a bowl, add the butter, and rub in with your fingertips until the mixture resembles fine breadcrumbs. Stir in the remaining sugar and the nuts.

❸ Sprinkle the crumble mixture over the fruit and bake in the preheated oven for 25 minutes, until the topping is golden and the fruit bubbling.

★ *Tip: For a change, try 1 lb 2 oz/500 g sliced cooking apples or dessert pears instead of the mixed berries.*

Whole grain per serving 2 | Serves 4 | Prep. time 35 mins

choc chip muffins

1¾ cups whole wheat flour
3 tsp baking powder
½ tsp salt
4 tbsp unsweetened cocoa
⅓ cup light brown sugar
½ cup milk or semisweet chocolate chips
¾ cup reduced-fat plain strained yogurt
generous ¾ cup lowfat or skim milk
1 large egg
1 large ripe banana
3 tbsp butter

❶ Preheat the oven to 400°F/200°C and line a 12-cup muffin pan with paper liners. Sift the flour, baking powder, salt, and cocoa into a bowl and stir in the sugar and chocolate chips.

❷ Beat together the yogurt, milk, and egg in another bowl. Mash the banana in a dish with a fork until almost liquid. Melt the butter in a saucepan over low heat and stir into the banana. Add the banana mixture to the yogurt mixture and stir well.

❸ Add the wet ingredients to the dry mixture and stir until just blended. Divide the mixture among the paper liners and bake in the preheated oven for 20 minutes, until risen and just firm to the touch. Transfer to a wire rack to cool.

Whole grain per muffin 1   Prep time 30 mins

mini oat cookies

low-calorie oil spray or vegetable oil, for brushing
8 tbsp butter, softened
generous ½ cup light brown sugar
1 large egg
1 tsp vanilla extract
¾ cup whole wheat flour
1 tsp baking powder
¼ tsp salt
⅔ cup rolled oats
2 shredded wheat biscuits, well crushed
6 tbsp lowfat or skim milk
scant ½ cup chopped plumped dried apricots
⅓ cup chopped mixed nuts

❶ Preheat the oven to 350°F/180°C and spray 2 baking sheets with low-calorie oil spray or brush lightly with oil. Preferably using an electric mixer, beat the butter and sugar together in a bowl until creamy.

❷ Beat in the egg and vanilla extract, sift in the flour, baking powder, and salt, then add all the remaining ingredients, and mix until thoroughly combined.

❸ Spoon level dessertspoonfuls of the mixture onto the prepared baking sheets, spacing them well apart, and bake in the preheated oven for 15 minutes, until golden. Let cool on a wire rack before eating—the cookies should be semisoft.

Whole grain per cookie 0.5

Prep. time 30 mins

banana cake

6 tbsp sunflower oil, plus extra for oiling
4 ripe bananas, mashed
⅓ cup Brazil nuts, coarsely chopped (see Tip)
4 tbsp water
⅔ cup raisins
1½ cups rolled oats
heaping 1 tbsp whole wheat flour
½ tsp vanilla extract

❶ Preheat the oven to 375°F/190°C. Oil and line a
8 x 4 x 2-inch/20 x 10 x 5-cm loaf pan with parchment paper.
Mix together all of the ingredients in a large bowl—the final
consistency should be soft and moist.

❷ Spoon the mixture into the prepared pan and bake in
the preheated oven for about 50 minutes, or until a skewer
inserted into the center comes out clean.

❸ Let cool in the pan for 10 minutes before turning out, then
let cool completely before slicing.

⭐ *Tip: You can omit the Brazil nuts, if you like, and add the same quantity
of chopped plumped dried dates or apricots instead.*

chocolate crispies

3½ oz/100 g milk chocolate
3½ oz/100 g semisweet chocolate
4½ tbsp butter
1 tbsp superfine sugar
4 shredded wheat biscuits
½ cup chopped nuts
1 tbsp candied cherries, chopped, or dried cranberries
  (see Tip)
vegetable oil, for brushing

❶ Break the chocolate into small pieces and put in a heatproof bowl with the butter. Set the bowl over a saucepan of gently simmering water (making sure the bowl doesn't touch the water) to melt. When the chocolate and butter have melted, stir in the sugar, then remove from the heat and let cool until just warm.

❷ Meanwhile, use your hands to break up the shredded wheat biscuits into fine strands, place in a bowl, and stir in the nuts and cherries. Lightly oil a baking sheet.

❸ Stir the just-warm chocolate into the shredded wheat biscuit mixture, then use your hands to mold it into 6 balls. Put them on the baking sheet and chill in the refrigerator for about 1 hour, until set.

⭐ *Tip: You could also use dried strawberries instead of the cherries or cranberries.*

Whole grain per crispie: 1   Makes: 6   Prep. time: 10 mins

raisin and date loaf

vegetable oil, for brushing
scant 1¾ cups whole wheat flour
1½ tsp baking powder
½ tsp salt
2 tbsp dark brown sugar
scant ½ cup raisins (see Tips)
heaping ½ cup chopped plumped dried pitted dates
2 tbsp honey
3 tbsp malt extract (see Tips)
⅔ cup lowfat or skim milk

❶ Preheat the oven to 350°F/180°C. Oil and line a 8 x 4 x 2-inch/ 20 x 10 x 5-cm loaf pan with parchment paper. Put the flour, baking powder, salt, sugar, raisins, and dates into a bowl and stir well.

❷ Heat the honey, malt extract, and milk in a small saucepan until the malt extract has melted, stirring well. Tip into the dry mixture and stir until combined, adding a little extra milk if necessary for a soft, dropping consistency.

❸ Spoon the mixture into the prepared pan and bake in the preheated oven for 1 hour, or until a skewer inserted into the center comes out clean. Let cool, then store in an airtight tin.

Tips: You can use any dried fruit instead of the raisins. Malt extract is widely available in jars. It can be bought at health or specialty food stores.

Whole grain per slice 1

Prep time 1 hour